Games
Around the World

Casey Null Petersen

Consultant

Timothy Rasinski, Ph.D.
Kent State University

Publishing Credits

Dona Herweck Rice, *Editor-in-Chief*

Robin Erickson, *Production Director*

Lee Aucoin, *Creative Director*

Conni Medina, M.A.Ed., *Editorial Director*

Jamey Acosta, *Editor*

Heidi Kellenberger, *Editor*

Lexa Hoang, *Designer*

Stephanie Reid, *Photo Editor*

Rachelle Cracchiolo, M.S.Ed., *Publisher*

Based on writing from *TIME For Kids*.

TIME For Kids and the *TIME For Kids* logo are registered trademarks of TIME Inc. Used under license.

Teacher Created Materials

5301 Oceanus Drive
Huntington Beach, CA 92649-1030
http://www.tcmpub.com
ISBN 978-1-4333-3653-9
© 2012 Teacher Created Materials, Inc.

Table of Contents

A World of Games

▲ children playing tag

All around the world, people play games. Many games have been handed down through the years. Others have traveled across seas and continents. Right now a child far away might be playing your favorite game.

young golf players ➤

▲ children playing tug-of-war

No matter who you are, there is a game for you to enjoy. So, come on…let's play!

Singing Games

The game London Bridge comes from England. To play, two children form a bridge with their arms. Those two players are the gatekeepers. Everyone sings "London Bridge" while the other players try to pass under the bridge before it comes down at the song's end. When caught, the player chooses to stand behind one of the gatekeepers. After everyone has been caught, the two teams have a **tug-of-war**. In Golden Bridge, the game is called Golden Bridge. Children in France play another version.

To play the game, children hold their hands together to make a bridge. Children pass under just as a ship passes under a bridge.

Did You Know?

London Bridge is played in Latin America, too. Here are the Spanish words in English.

Here's a woman (or man) selling figs,
Selling figs, selling figs,
Here's a woman selling figs,
Here she comes.
Now the figs she has sold,
She has sold, she has sold,
Now the figs she has sold,
Here she comes.

London Bridge

In Greece, children play Ringel Ringel. It is a lot like **Ring Around the Rosie**, one of the first games children in the United States learn to play. In fact, children play some form of this game in nearly every country.

It's All Greek to Me

Here are the words to Ringel Ringel in English. When children get to *hush, hush, hush*, they all squat down.

Ringel, Ringel, ring-o!
See the children three-o,
Sitting by the lilac bush.
Call together, hush, hush, hush!

▼ a painting of children playing Ring Around the Rosie

▲ a rose tree

▲ Children play jump rope in many countries.

Children around the world play **jump rope**. There are often songs and chants to go with the jump rope moves. For example, in South America, children play **The Clock**. To play, two children turn the ropes. The first jumper runs through or jumps without being touched by the rope. The players count "Zero!" The next runs in, jumps once, and runs out as the players count "One!" The next jumps two times, and this continues until the rope touches a player.

Children in Ukraine take turns doing fancier and fancier jumps until someone gets caught in the rope.

A different chanting game is played in the United States. In **Red Rover**, players chant "Red Rover, Red Rover, let (name) come over!" The called player rushes to break through the joined arms of the opposite team. If successful, the player takes someone from that team to join his or her team. If not, the player must join the other team. In Russia, the game is called Pioneer.

Everybody Clap!

We really don't know how long people have been playing clapping games, but **historians** think they go back a very long time. Clapping games are usually played with two players who sing or chant to a rhythm of claps.

Running and Jumping Games

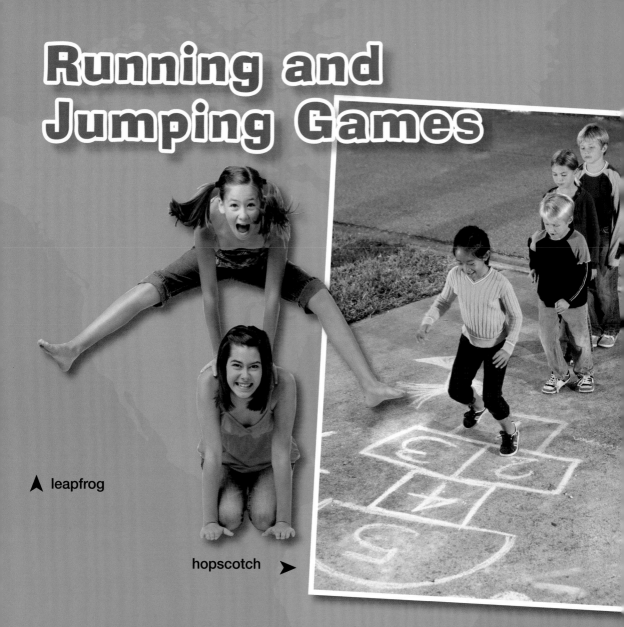

▲ leapfrog

hopscotch ▶

Hopscotch has been played for thousands of years. In South Africa, children play it on rectangles drawn in the dirt. They hop on one foot, place a stone in one of the rectangles, and kick the stone with the same foot!

The Excited Burro is a game from Cuba. Burro (BOOR-oh) is the Spanish word for donkey. The "burro" stoops over so that the other players can jump over him, as in **leapfrog**. As players take turns jumping, they say and do different things. The Excited Burro is just one way to play leapfrog. Children around the world play it in many different ways.

Playing The Excited Burro in the United States

If you were playing The Excited Burro in the United States, you might use the words below. When you reach twelve, everyone runs, and the "burro" tries to catch them.

At one, what fun!
At two, my shoe.
At three, my tea.
At four, my door.
At five, man alive!
    (This player pokes the "burro.")
At six, no more tricks.
At seven, near to heaven.
At eight, put it straight.
    (This player puts a handkerchief
    on the burro's back.)
At nine, now it's mine.
    (This player takes the handkerchief.)
At ten, a tiny hen.
At eleven, over again.
At twelve...run!

Do you like to play tag? In Brazil, children play a fun tag game called **Cat Meow**. One child, called "It," is blindfolded while the other players **scatter**. When It finds someone, he or she demands, "Cat, meow!" The player meows, and It tries to guess who the player is.

▲ There are many kinds of relays.
This is a running relay.

Carrying Baskets is a **relay** game played in Africa and Asia. Players balance small baskets on their heads and race to the finish line. If players touch or drop the basket, it is back to the start for them!

Playing with This and That

Backgammon and checkers are popular almost everywhere. Similar games were played in ancient (EYN-shunt) Egypt and Greece. Chess may have begun in Iran and then spread to the rest of the world.

➤ Children playing checkers in Mexico.

Coin Toss

Have you ever flipped a coin for heads or tails? Toss a Coin is an African game that is played the same way. However, small, smooth stones are used. They are wet or shiny on one side and dry or dull on the other.

▲ Mongolian boys
playing jacks

Did You Know?

Jacks used to be called knucklebones because jacks were made of stones or bones! The song "This Old Man" comes from the game of jacks. Do you remember the line "Knick knack paddywack, give a dog a bone"?

▼ American jacks

Jacks is an old game that is played all over the world. Long ago, jacks were used for fortune telling. Now children play a game with them by picking up pieces while bouncing a small ball.

Jewish children from Israel and around the world play the **dreidel** (DREYD-l) game at **Hanukkah**. The dreidel is a special top with **Hebrew** letters. Each player begins with the same number of counters, usually candy or coins. On his or her turn, a player spins the dreidel. Each letter tells the player to do something different with his or her counters.

Yo-Yo

The yo-yo, which is really just a top spinning on a string, is thought to be the second oldest toy ever made. The oldest is probably the doll.

Did You Know?

The world's biggest yo-yo was built in 2010. It is over 11 feet tall.

Tops

Nobody knows for sure when the first tops were spun. The dreidel has been around for more than 2,000 years. Top games have been played in China for centuries.

a boy playing with a ➤ wooden top

Marbles was first played by ancient Egyptians using clay marbles. Italian children were the first to play with glass marbles. The game of marbles is played by **flicking** one marble, called a shooter, into a circle filled with other marbles in order to hit some of them out of the circle.

Cat's Cradle may have been invented by American Indians. To play, one or more players weaves a circle of string through and around their fingers and wrists in order to make shapes and designs. Sometimes the designs tell a story.

Some people think **Pick Up Sticks** was invented in China. Others say American Indians invented it. Thin colored sticks are dropped into a pile. Each stick has a different **value** (VAL-yoo). Players must take away one stick at a time without touching or moving any of the others. It's tricky to do!

The Oldest Game

Mancala (man-KAWL-uh), the African stone game, is thought to be the oldest game in the world. Throughout Africa, Asia, the Middle East, the Indies, the Philippines, and even South America, the game has been played by everyone. Mancala comes from an Arab word that means "to move."

On the Map

Can you find all the games and places in this book? Take a look!

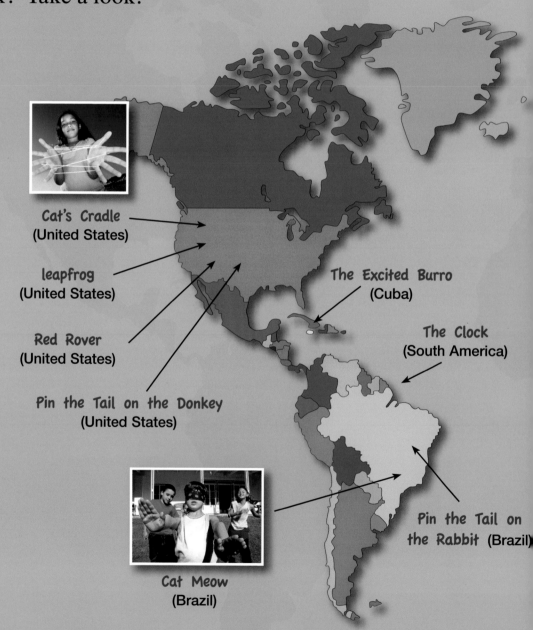

Cat's Cradle
(United States)

leapfrog
(United States)

Red Rover
(United States)

Pin the Tail on the Donkey
(United States)

The Excited Burro
(Cuba)

The Clock
(South America)

Pin the Tail on
the Rabbit (Brazil)

Cat Meow
(Brazil)

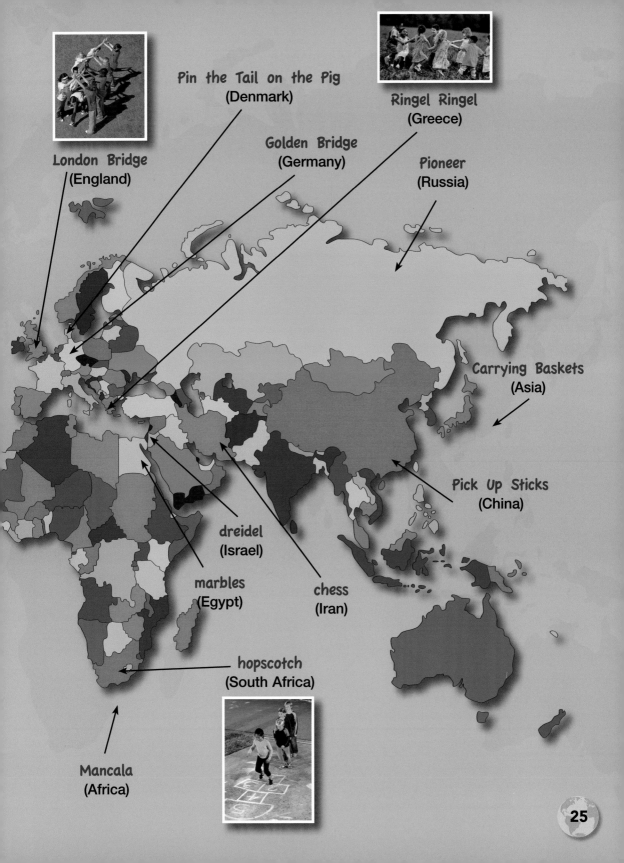

London Bridge
(England)

Pin the Tail on the Pig
(Denmark)

Golden Bridge
(Germany)

Ringel Ringel
(Greece)

Pioneer
(Russia)

Carrying Baskets
(Asia)

Pick Up Sticks
(China)

dreidel
(Israel)

marbles
(Egypt)

chess
(Iran)

hopscotch
(South Africa)

Mancala
(Africa)

Something for Everyone

What's your favorite game? There's something for everyone. Do you like quiet games? How about chess? Do you like noisy games? How about tag? Choose a game, and let's play!

Glossary

ancient—very, very old

backgammon—a game played by two players with checker-like pieces on a gameboard

Carrying Baskets—a game in which players race to the finish line while balancing baskets on their heads

Cat Meow—a game with a child called "It" who is blindfolded and tries to find the other players

Cat's Cradle—a game with two players who make puzzles for each other out of a long piece of string

checkers—a board game with two players who try to collect each other's pieces

chess—a strategy game with two players who try to capture each other's "king" piece

Clock, The—a game played in South America by jumping over a rope

dreidel—a special top with Hebrew letters

Excited Burro, The—a game played by leaping over the back of the person in front of you

flicking—the hand motion used to move the shooter marble

Hanukkah—an eight-day festival celebrated by the Jewish people

Hebrew—the language of the Jewish people

historians—experts on history who study and write about past events

hopscotch—a counting game played by hopping onto numbers drawn on the ground

jacks—a game played by bouncing a small ball and trying to pick up jacks while the ball is in the air

jump rope—a game played by jumping over a long rope turned by players at each end

leapfrog—a game played by leaping over the back of the person in front of you

marbles—a game played by shooting a large ball at smaller balls

Pick Up Sticks—a game played by pulling one stick out of a pile without moving the other sticks around it

Red Rover—a game in which two teams try to break through the joined arms of the opposite team

relay—to pass from one person to another

Ring Around the Rosie—a game played by joining hands in a circle and spinning

scatter—to separate and move suddenly in many different directions

tug-of-war—a sporting event or game with two teams pulling at opposite ends of a rope

value—how much something is worth

Index